Biography

James Egan was born in 1985 and grew up in
Portarlington, Co. Laois in the Midlands of Ireland.
In 2008, James moved to England and studied in Oxford.
James married his wife in 2012 and currently lives in
Havant in Hampshire.
James had his first book, 365 Ways to Stop Sabotaging
Your Life, published in 2014.
Several of James' books have become No.1 Best Sellers
in the UK including 1000 Facts about Horror Movies,
3000 Facts About the Greatest Movies Ever, 365 Things
People Believe That Aren't True, Another 365 Things
People Believe That Aren't True, and 500 Things People
Believe That Aren't True.

Books by James Egan
Fairytale
Inherit the Earth
Inherit the Earth: The Animal Kingdom
1000 Facts About the United States
Words That Need to Exist in English
Hilarious Things That Kids Say
Hilarious Things That Mums Say
1000 Facts about TV Shows Vol. 1-3
1000 Facts about Animated Shows Vol. 1-3
1000 Facts about Actors Vol. 1-3
1000 Facts about Countries Vol. 1-3
Dinosaurs Had Feathers (and other Random Facts)
1000 Facts about Animals Vol. 1-3
1000 Facts about James Bond
1000 Inspiring Facts
How to Psychologically Survive Cancer
1000 Out-of-this-World Facts about Space
1000 Facts about the Greatest Movies Ever Vol. 1-3
1000 Facts about Film Directors
1000 Facts about Superhero Movies Vol. 1-3
1000 Facts about Superheroes Vol. 1-3
1000 Facts about Supervillains Vol. 1-3
1000 Facts about Comic Books Vol. 1-3
1000 Facts about Animated Films Vol. 1-3
1000 Facts about Horror Movies Vol. 1-3
1000 Facts about American Presidents
Adorable Animal Facts
1000 Facts about Video Games Vol. 1-3
Things People Believe That Aren't True Vol. 1-4
1000 Fact about Film Director
The Mega Misconception Book
3000 Astounding Quotes
1000 Facts About Comic Book Characters Vol. 1-3
100 Classic Stories in 100 Pages
500 Facts about Godzilla
365 Ways to Stop Sabotaging Your Life
Flat Earthers Around the Globe
1000 Facts about Historic Figures Vol. 1-3
1000 Facts About Writers
1000 Facts about Ireland
The Biggest Movie Plotholes
1000 Facts about the Human Body

1,000 Amazing Quotes

By

James Egan

ISBN: 9781326390839

Because of the dynamic nature of the Internet, any web addresses or links contained in this book may have changed since publication and may no longer be valid. The views expressed in this work are solely those of the author and do not necessarily reflect the views of the publisher, and the publisher hereby disclaims any responsibility for them.

Any people depicted in stock imagery provided by Thinkstock are models, and such images are being used for illustrative purposes only.
Certain stock imagery © Thinkstock.

Lulu Publishing Services rev. date: 13/08/2015

Dedicated to
Mark Hooper

For all of his inspiration and kindness
throughout the years

1. Affairs are easier of entrance than of exit;
   and it is but common prudence to see our
   way out before we venture in.

   - Aesop

2. A groom spent long hours combing and
   clipping the horse he charged but daily stole
   a portion of his oats to sell for profit.
   The horse got into a bad condition and at last
   cried,
   "If you want me to look sleek and well, you
   must comb me less and feed me more."

   - Aesop

3. Have I played the part well?
   Then applaud as I exit.
   - Augustus, last words of the first Roman
   Emperor

4. You get what you want in life, but not your
   second choice too.

   – Alison Lurie

5. Letting the cat out of the bag is a lot easier
   than putting it back in.

   - Will Rogers

6. Evil is whatever distracts.

   - Franz Kafka

7. An appeaser is one who feeds a crocodile –
   hoping it will feed him last.
   - Winston Churchill

8. Now I am become Death, the destroyer of
   worlds.
   - J. Robert Oppenheimer (father of the atomic
             bomb) upon witnessing the first tests

9. A hen is heavy when carried far.
   - Irish Proverb

10.   The one who loves the least, controls the
   relationship.
   - Robert Anthony

11.   A hound's food is in its legs.
   - Irish Proverb

12.   Anyone who cannot come to terms with
   his life while he is alive needs one hand to
   ward off a little his despair over his fate…
   but with his other hand, he can note down
   what he sees among the ruins.
   - Franz Kafka

13.   There comes a time when you have to
   stop crossing oceans for people who won't
   even jump a puddle for you.
   - Anon

14.   A man is not honest simply because he never had a chance to steal.

- Yiddish Proverb

15.   Men deal with life, as children with their play
Who first misuse, then cast their toys away.

- William Cowper

16.   A man may well bring a horse to the water, but he cannot make him drink.

- John Heywood

17.   Most people are other people.
Their thoughts are someone else's opinions, their lives a mimicry, their passions a quotation.

- Oscar Wilde

18.   A man should live if only to satisfy his curiosity.

- Yiddish Proverb

19.   Believing in progress does not mean believing that any progress is made.

- Franz Kafka

20.   The brain is wider than the sky.

- Emily Dickinson

21.　It's not whether you get knocked down, it's whether you get up.

　　　　　　　　　- Vince Lombardi

22.　A new broom sweeps clean, but the old brush knows all the corners.

　　　　　　　　　- Irish Proverb

23.　A rumor goes in one ear and out many mouths.

　　　　　　　　　- Chinese Proverb

24.　A society grows great when old men plant trees whose shade they known they shall never sit in.

　　　　　　　　　- Greek Proverb

25.　A silent mouth is melodious.

　　　　　　　　　- Irish Proverb

26.　Success is a lousy teacher. It seduces smart people into thinking they can't lose.

　　　　　　　　　- Bill Gates

27.　If a man with experience meets a man with money, the experienced man gets the money and the formally rich man gets an experience.

　　　　　　　　　- Anon

28. I don't believe in astrology; I'm a Sagittarius, and we're skeptical.

 - Arthur C. Clarke

29. Behind every argument is someone's ignorance.

 - Robert Benchley

30. A perfect relationship isn't ever actually perfect, it's just one where both people never give up.

 - Anon

31. A soft answer turneth away wrath: but grievous words stir up anger.

 - Bible - Proverbs 15:1

32. A spoon does not know the taste of soup, nor a learned fool the taste of wisdom.

 - Welsh Proverb

33. You can fool some of the people all of the time, you can fool all of the people some of the time but you can never fool all of the people all of the time.

 - Abraham Lincoln

34. Happiness is a by-product, not a goal.

 - Eleanor Roosevelt

35. Never befriend one who's not better than thyself.

- Confucius

36. A son is a son till he gets him a wife,
But a daughter's a daughter the rest of your life.

- Anon

37. Anger is never without an argument, but seldom with a good one.

- Indira Gandhi

38. A thief believes everybody steals.

- Anon

39. A thorn defends the rose, harming those who would steal the blossom.

- Chinese Proverb

40. You can't move so fast that you try to change the mores faster than people can accept it. That doesn't mean you do nothing, but it means that you do the things that need to be done according to the priority.

- Eleanor Roosevelt

41. Cleverness is not wisdom.

- Euripides

42.   The hardest thing in the world to understand is income taxes.

>   - Albert Einstein

43.   The universe is under no obligation to make sense to you.

>   - Neil de Grasse Tyson

44.   The best of seers is he who guesses well.

>   - Euripides

45.   Nothing contributes so much to tranquilize the mind as a steady purpose - a point on which the soul may fix its intellectual eye.

>   - Mary Shelley

46.   When you dance, your purpose is not to get to a certain place on the floor. It's to enjoy each step along the way.

>   - Wayne Dyer

47.   I do not wish women to have power over men; but over themselves.

>   - Mary Shelley

48.   Happiness is brief. God batters its sails.

>   - Euripides

49. There are mysteries which men can only guess at, which age by age they may solve only in part.

- Bram Stoker

50. Technology is just a tool. In terms of getting the kids working together and motivating them, the teacher is the most important.

- Bill Gates

51. A throne is only a bench covered in velvet.

- French Proverb

52. If you change the way you look at things, the things you look at change.

- Wayne Dyer

53. Fashion is a form of ugliness so intolerable, we have to update it every six months.

- Oscar Wilde

54. A tree falls the way it leans.

- Bulgarian Proverb

55. If you can't make it good, at least make it look good.

- Bill Gates

56.   Only three types of people tell the truth; kids, drunk people and anyone who is really really angry.

- Richard Pryor

57.   He who lives by the sword, dies by the sword.

- Jesus Christ

58.   My life is my message.

- Mahatma Gandhi

59.   Invention, it must be humbly admitted, does not consist in creating out of void, but out of chaos.

- Mary Shelley

60.   To love beauty is to see light.

- Victor Hugo

61.   We humans have millions of years of evolutionary baggage that makes us regard competition in a deadly light.

- Vernor Vinge

62.   A wise man hears one word and understands two.

- Yiddish Proverb

63. Nobody wants to hear this, but sometimes the person you want most is the person you're best without.

          - Anon

64. If a writer knows enough about what he is writing about, he may omit things that he knows. The dignity of movement of an iceberg is due to only one ninth of it being above water.

          - Ernest Hemingway

65. My dreams were all my own; I accounted for them to nobody; they were my refuge when annoyed – my dearest pleasure when free.

          - Mary Shelley

66. He is rich who rejoices in his portion.

          - Benjamin Franklin

67. A wise man makes his own decisions, an ignorant man follows the public opinion.

          - Chinese Proverb

68. A man who does not trust himself will never really trust anybody.

          - Jean-Francois Paul de Gondi,
                    Cardinal de Retz
                    (Memoires)

69. Politeness has become so rare that some people mistake it for flirtation.

- Anon

70. Being ignorant is not so much a shame, as being unwilling to learn.

- Benjamin Franklin

71. A worth woman is far more precious than jewels; strength and dignity are her clothing.

- Bible – Proverbs 31

72. Advice should be viewed from behind.

- Swedish Proverb

73. If you reveal your secrets to the wind, you should blame the wind for revealing them to the trees.

- Khali Gibran

74. Act in the valley so that you need not fear those who stand on the hill.

- Danish Proverb

75. And those who were seen dancing were thought to be insane by those who could not hear the music.

- Friedrich Nietzsche

76.   By all means let's be open-minded, but not so open-minded that our brains drop out.
                                  - Richard Dawkins

77.   I've always been more comfortable sinking while clutching a good theory than swimming with an ugly fact.
                                  - David Mamet

78.   Education is learning what you didn't even know you didn't know.
                                  - Daniel J. Boorstin

79.   All things grow with time, except grief.
                                  - Yiddish Proverb

80.   We are at our most destructive when we think we are indestructible.
                                  - Mike Fisher

81.   There is no rule on how to write. Sometimes it comes easily and perfectly; sometimes it's like drilling rock and then blasting it out with charges.
                                  - Ernest Hemingway

82.   We do not see things as they are, we see things as we are.
                                  - Anon

83. Attraction is beyond our will or ideas sometimes.

- Juliette Binoche

84. A dream is what makes people love life even when it is painful.

- Theodore Zeldin

85. An angry man is not fit to pray.

- Yiddish Proverb

86. No man ever believes that the Bible means what it says; he is always convinced that it says what he means.

- George Bernard Shaw

87. An enemy will agree, but a friend will argue.

- Russian Proverb

88. But O, how bitter a thing it is to look into happiness through another man's eyes.

- William Shakespeare

89. Don't burn your bed to catch a flea.

- Turkish Proverb

90. An old rat is a brave rat.

- French Proverb

91.   Anger can be an expensive luxury.

- Italian Proverb

92.   When you judge another, you do not define them, you define yourself.

- Wayne Dyer

93.   I do sometimes accuse people of ignorance, but that is not intended to be an insult. I'm ignorant of lots of things. Ignorance is sometimes what can be remedied by education.

- Richard Dawkins

94.   Each person is an enigma. You're a puzzle not only to yourself but also to everyone else, and the great mystery of our time is how we penetrate this puzzle.

- Theodore Zeldin

95.   People will question all the good things they hear about you but believe all the bad without a second thought.

- Anon

96.   Falling in love is not at all the most stupid thing that people do but gravitation cannot be held responsible for it.

- Albert Einstein

97. Haste is blind.

> - Titus Livius

98. We should strive to be employed in such a way that we don't realize that what we're doing is work.

> - Theodore Zeldin

99. People who want the most approval get the least.

> - Wayne Dyer

100. To idolize a person means you don't get to know them, and the idea that you can become one is a myth, and it also means that you don't need to talk to one another because you're the same person.

> - Theodore Zeldin

101. He who displays himself does not shine. He who stands on his toes does not stand well.

> – Chinese Proverb

102. A wise girl kisses but doesn't love, listens but doesn't believe, and leaves before she is left.

> - Marilyn Monroe

103. No man is justified in doing evil on the
   ground of expedience.

> \- Theodore Roosevelt

104. Anger is as a stone cast into a wasp's
   nest.

> \- Malabr Proverb

105. A thing of beauty is a joy forever, its
   loveliness increases, it will never pass into
   nothingness.

> \- John Keats

106. I used to think that the worst thing in life
   was to end up all alone.
   It's not. The worst thing in life is ending up
   with people who make you feel alone.

> \- Robin Williams

107. The components of anxiety, stress, fear
   and anger do not exist independently of you
   in the world. They simply do not exist in the
   physical world, even though we talk about
   them as if they do.

> \- Wayne Dyer

108. The one who boasts will only gain one
   thing: enemies.

> \- Anon

109. And it seems to me important for a country, for a nation to certainly know about its glorious achievements but also to know where its ideals failed, in order to keep that from happening again.

> - George Takei

110. If a child can't learn the way we teach, maybe we should teach the way we learn.

> - Michael J. Fox

111. He who vaunts himself does not find his merit acknowledged.

> – Chinese Proverb

112. Your most unhappy customers are your greatest source of learning.

> - Bill Gates

113. If science proves some belief of Buddhism wrong, then Buddhism will have to change.

> - Dalai Lama

114. You have brains in your head. You have feet in your shoes. You can steer yourself in any direction you choose. You're on your own, and you know what you know. And you are the guy who'll decide where to go.

> - Dr. Seuss

115. Whom the gods wish to destroy, they first call promising.

> – Cyril Connolly
> (Enemies of Promise)

116. Just because you're offended, doesn't mean you're right.

> - Ricky Gervais

117. Every hero becomes a bore at last.

> – Ralph Emerson

118. I don't care what you think about me, I don't think about you at all.

> - Jack Nicholson

119. People ask you for criticism, but they only want praise.

> – W. Somerset Maugham

120. Change will not come if we wait for some other person or some other time. We are the ones we've been waiting for. We are the change that we seek.

> - Barack Obama

121. As a dog returneth to his vomit, so a fool returneth to his folly.

> - Bible - Proverbs 26:11

122. Don't cry because it's over. Smile because it happened.

- Dr. Seuss

123. I've always tried to go a step past wherever people expected me to end up.

- Beverly Sills

124. Normal is getting dressed in clothes that you buy for work and driving through traffic in a car that you are still paying for – in order to get to the job you need to pay for the clothes and the car, and the house you leave vacant all day so you can afford to live in it.

- Ellen Goodman

125. As a man thinketh in his heart, so is he.

- Bible – Proverbs 23:7

126. Compliments cost nothing, yet many pay dear for them.

- Thomas Fuller

127. If you can't explain it simply, you don't understand it well enough.

- Albert Einstein

128. Always write angry letters to your enemies. Never mail them.

- James Fallows

129. Destiny can justify a tyrant's authority for crime or a fool's excuse for failure.

- Ambrose Bierce

130. Respect your parents. They passed school without Google.

- Anon

131. Climb mountains to see lowlands.

- Chinese Proverb

132. Darkness reigns at the foot of the lighthouse.

- Japanese Proverb

133. I not only use all the brains that I have, but all that I can borrow.

- Woodrow Wilson

134. The more you praise and celebrate your life, the more there is in life to celebrate.

- Oprah Winfrey

135. The more that you read, the more things you will know. The more that you learn, the more places you'll go.

- Dr. Seuss

136. Children are poor men's riches.

- English Proverb

137. In the last few years, the very idea of telling the truth, the whole truth, and nothing but the truth is dredged up only as a final resort when the alternative options of deception, threat and bribery have all been exhausted.

- Michael Musto

138. Failure is another stepping stone to greatness.

- Oprah Winfrey

139. Deal with the faults of others as gently as with your own.

- Chinese Proverb

140. Sometimes legends make reality, and become more useful than the facts.

- Salman Rushdie

141. Surround yourself with only people who are going to lift you higher.

- Oprah Winfrey

142. As cold waters to a thirsty soul, so is good news from a far country.

- Bible – Proverbs 25:25

143. Better give a penny then lend twenty.

- Italian Proverb

144. He has all the virtues I dislike and none
of the vices I admire.

- Winston Churchill

145. He who permits himself to tell a lie once,
finds it much easier to do it a second and a
third time till at length it becomes habitual.

- Thomas Jefferson

146. Everyone wants to be successful until
they see what it actually takes.

- Anon

147. I like nonsense, it wakes up the brain
cells. Fantasy is a necessary ingredient in
living, it's a way of looking at life through
the wrong end of a telescope. Which is what
I do, and that enables you to laugh at life's
realities.

- Dr. Seuss

148. You get fat if you take in more calories
than you burn. That's simple science.
Everybody knows this. It doesn't sneaky up
on you. It's a fact.

-Ricky Gervais

149. A people free to choose will always
choose peace.

- Ronald Reagan

150. Death always comes too early or too late.

- English Proverb

151. If a single teacher can't teach all the subjects, then how can you expect a single student to learn all subjects?

- Anon

152. It is less shameful for a king to be overcome by force of arms than by bribery.

- Sallust

153. I don't understand why people think that having a gay child means they failed as a parent. Disowning your child means you failed as a parent.

- Anon

154. Death closes all doors.

- English Proverb

155. Do not look where you fell but where you slipped.

- African Proverb

156. Do not rejoice at my grief, for when mine is old, yours will be new.

- Spanish Proverb

157. You have a choice - you either joined or
formed a gang or you let others bully you.
- Jack Bowman

158. Do not talk Arabic in the house of a
Moor.
- Oriental Proverb

159. Yes, evolution is a theory. Gravity is just
a theory too. Anyone who doubts it is
welcome to jump out of a ten-story window.
- Richard Dawkins

160. You can discover what your enemy fears
most by observing the means he uses to
frighten you.
– Eric Hoffer

161. A bee is never as busy as it seems; it's
just that it can't buzz any slower.
- Kin Hubbard

162. Normal is an illusion. What is normal for
the spider is chaos for the fly.
- Morticia Addams
(The Addams Family)

163. True reconciliation does not consist in
merely forgetting the past.
- Nelson Mandela

164. It can't be something that you're doing to lose weight, and then once you do, you're done. I do it every day of my life.

- LeAnn Rimes

165. You'd never invite a thief into your house. So why would you allow thoughts that steal your joy to makes themselves at home in your mind?

- Anon

166. No weapon has ever settled a moral problem. It can impose a solution but it cannot guarantee it to be a just one.

- Ernest Hemingway

167. Those who don't study history are doomed to repeat it. Yet those who study history are doomed to stand by helplessly while everyone else repeats it.

- Anon

168. For me context is the key - from that comes the understanding of everything.

- Kenneth Noland

169. Death pays all debts.

- English Proverb

170. If you think adventure is dangerous, try routine, it's lethal.

- Paulo Coelho

171. It seems to me that everything that happens to us is a disconcerting mix of choice and contingency.

- Penelope Lively

172. We all have that one friend who always gives relationship advice but is still single.

- Anon

173. The components to power are those who- Want it, Give it, Control it.

- Anon

174. The strength of the pack is the wolf, and strength of the wolf is the pack.

– Rudyard Kipling

175. All the war-propaganda, all the screaming and lies and hatred, comes invariably from people who are not fighting.

- George Orwell

176. The opposite of talking should be listening, not waiting.

- Anon

177. It's never your successful friends posting the inspirational quotes.

          - Damien Fahey

178. It is the province of knowledge to speak and it is the privilege of wisdom to listen.

          - Oliver Wendell Holmes

179. Holding a grudge is letting someone live rent-free in your head.

          - Anon

180. The world is an oyster, but you don't crack it open on a mattress.

          – Arthur Miller

181. The discovery of a new dish does more for human happiness than the discovery of a star.

          - Anthelme Brillat-Savarin
          (The Physiology of Taste)

182. Do not speak of secrets in a field that is full of little hills.

          - Hebrew Proverb

183. The best sign of a healthy relationship is no sign of it online.

          - Anon

184. Tell me what you eat, and I will tell you what you are.

- Anon

185. Do not use a hatchet to remove a fly from your friend's forehead.

- Chinese Proverb

186. All books are divisible into two classes, the books of the hour, and the books of all time.

- John Ruskin

187. Hesitation increases in relation to risk in equal proportion to age.

- Ernest Heminway

188. Cooking is the most ancient of the arts, for Adam was born hungry.

– Anthelme Brillat-Savarin
(The Physiology of Taste)

189. Don't imitate the fly before you have wings.

- French Proverb

190. If one does not know to which port is sailing, no wind is favorable.

- Lucius Annaeus Seneca

191. Even a small thorn causes festering.
- Irish Proverb

192. Everyone is kneaded out of the same dough but not baked in the same oven.
- Yiddish Proverb

193. Never think that war, no matter how necessary, nor how justified, is not a crime.
- Ernest Hemingway

194. He that gives good advice, builds with one hand; he that gives good counsel and example, build with both; but he that gives good admonition and bad example, builds with one hand and pulls down with the other.
- Francis Bacon

195. Most people return great favors with one thing – ingratitude.
- Benjamin Franklin

196. God created war so that Americans would learn geography.
- Mark Twain

197. Nothing gives one person so much advantage over another as to remain always cool and unruffled under all circumstances.
- Thomas Jefferson

198. If you're not careful, the newspapers will have you hating the people who are being oppressed, and loving the people who are doing the oppressing.

- Malcolm Little

199. Celebrities who have plastic surgery don't look younger or more attractive. They just look like people who had plastic surgery.

– Kate Winslet

200. Everyone loves justice in the affairs of another.

- Italian Proverb

201. I always wondered why somebody didn't do something about that, then I realized I am somebody.

- Anon

202. Everyone pushes a falling fence.

- Chinese Proverb

203. Experience is a comb which nature gives to men when they are bald.

- Eastern Proverb

204. I don't need the fillers and additives to taint the natural goodness of real food.

- Mark Hyman

205. Credit goes to the man who convinces the world, not the man whom the idea first occurs.

- Franic Darwin

206. I love rumors. I always find out amazing things about myself I never knew.

- Anon

207. A prudent question is one-half of wisdom.

- Francis Bacon

208. Not knowing when the dawn will come, I open ever door.

- Emily Dickinson

209. It's amazing what you can accomplish if you don't care who gets the credit.

- Harry Truman

210. By imposing too great a responsibility or rather all of it, you crush yourself.

- Franz Kafka

211. A word is dead when it is said, some say. I say it just begins to live that day.

- Emily Dickinson

212. Someone needs to explain to me why wanting clean drinking water makes you an activist, and why proposing to destroy water with chemical warfare doesn't make a corporation a terrorist.

- Winona Laduke

213. When you gradually add in nutrient-dense, fiber-rich foods, you simply stop feeling cravings. Instead of craving, you feel full, fulfilled, and content.

- Kathy Freston

214. Silence can be the worst criticism.

- Charles Buxton

215. I don't know how people can fake whole relationships. I can't even fake a hello to somebody I don't like.

- Anon

216. If your parents didn't leave you when you were young, then don't leave them when they are old.

- Anon

217. The trouble with having an open mind, of course, is that people will insist on coming along and trying to put things in it.

- Terry Pratchett

218. Proximity to power deludes some into thinking they wield it.

- Frank Underwood
(House of Cards)

219. Don't despair, not even over the fact that you don't despair.

- Franz Kafka

220. Damaged people are the most dangerous kind, because they already know they can survive.

- Anon

221. In 100 or 200 years' time, we may look back on the way we treat animals today as something like we today look back on the way our forefathers treated slaves.

- Richard Dawkins

222. We should feel sorrow, but not sink under its oppression.

- Confucius

223. I learned never to empty the well of my writing, but always to stop when there was still something there in the deep part of the well, and let it refill at night from the springs that fed it.

- Ernest Hemingway

224. The superior man acts before he speaks, and afterwards speaks according to his action.

- Kong Qiu

225. The superior man understands what is right; the inferior man understands what will sell.

- Chinese Proverb

226. As far as eating is concerned, humans are the most stupid animals on the planet. We kill billions of wild animals to protect the animals that we eat. We are destroying our environment to feed to the animals we eat. We spend more time, money and resources fattening up the animals that we eat, than we do feeding humans who are dying of hunger. The greatest irony is that after all the expense of raising these animals, we eat them; and they kill us slowly. And rather than recognize this madness, we torture and murder millions of other animals trying to find cures to disease caused by eating animals in the first place.

- Mike Anderson

227. Earth provides enough to satisfy every man's needs, but not every man's greed.

- Mahatma Gandhi

228. Hatred is self-punishment.

> \- Hosea Ballou

229. There is no friend as loyal as a book.

> \- Ernest Hemingway

230. When you cease to make a contribution, you begin to die.

> \- Eleanor Roosevelt

231. The superior man is modest in his speech, but exceeds in his actions.

> \- Confucius

232. The cruelest lies are told in silence.

> \- Adlai Stevenson

233. The best propaganda is more propaganda.

> \- Edward Bernays

234. An oppressive government is more to be feared than a tiger.

> \- Confucius

235. My experience has been that work is almost the best way to pull oneself out of the depths.

> \- Eleanor Roosevelt

236. If I read a book and it makes my whole body so cold, no fire can ever warm me, I know that is poetry.

- Emily Dickinson

237. If all insects on Earth disappeared, within 50 years all life on Earth would end. If human beings disappeared from the Earth, within 50 years all forms of life would flourish.

- Jonas Salk

238. To be wronged is nothing unless you continue to remember it.

- Kong Qiu

239. Be thankful for what you have; you'll end up having more. If you concentrate on what you don't have, you will never, ever have enough.

- Oprah Winfrey

240. Fortune is a woman: if you neglect her today do not expect to regain her tomorrow.

- French Proverb

241. Everything you are against weakens you. Everything you are for empowers you.

- Wayne Dyer

242. I don't think of myself as a poor deprived ghetto girl who made good. I think of myself as somebody who from an early age knew I was responsible for myself and I had to make good.

- Oprah Winfrey

243. Never before have humans been so ambitious, have they thought that they could be much more than their parents were.

- Theodore Zeldin

244. Good wine ruins the purse, and bad wine ruins the stomach.

- English Proverb

245. Flattery makes friends and truth makes enemies.

- Spanish Proverb

246. Greediness burst the bag.

- American Proverb

247. It's not how much we have, but how much we enjoy.

- Charles Spurgeon

248. What can't be cured must be endured.

- English Proverb

249. Where there is no struggle, there is no strength.

- Oprah Winfrey

250. Half a loaf is better than none.

- English Proverb

251. Grumbling makes the loaf no larger.

- English Proverb

252. You can get help from teachers, but you are going to have to learn a lot by yourself, sitting alone in a room.

- Dr. Seuss

253. Better to be poor and healthy rather than rich and sick.

- American Proverb

254. A savage is not the one who lives in the forest, but the one who destroys it.

- Anon

255. To be nameless in worthy deeds exceeds an infamous history.

- Sir Thomas Browne

256. A critic is a bundle of biases held loosely together by a sense of taste.

- Whitney Balliett

257. The most dangerous untruths are truths moderately distorted.
                    - George Christoph Lichtenberg

258. Critics, like eunuchs know how it works but they can't do it themselves.
                    - Anon

259. Cruelty, like every other vice, requires no motive outside of itself; it only requires opportunity.
                    - George Eliot

260. Are all men in disguise except those crying?
                    - Dannie Abse

261. Cruelty would be delicious if one could only find some sort of cruelty that didn't really hurt.
                    - George Bernard Shaw

262. The first voice which I uttered was crying, as all others do.
                    - Solomon Ibn Gabirol

263. A good metaphor can make any idea look good.
                    - Scott Adams

264. The garden is beautiful without filling it
with fairies.

                              - William Occam

265. Depression is frozen anger.
                              - Sigmund Freud

266. Without forgiveness, life is governed…
an endless cycle of resentment and
retaliation.

                              - Roberto Assagioli

267. To be angry with the right person and to
the right degree and at the right time and for
the right purpose, and in the right way – that
is not easy.

                              - Aristotle

268. The pleasures arising from thinking and
learning will make us think and learn all the
more.

                              - Aristotle

269. A friend to all is a friend to none.
                              - Aristotle

270. Beauty is a short-lived tyranny.
                              - Socrates

271. It is not part of true culture to tame tigers, any more than it is to make sheep ferocious.

- Henry David Thoreau

272. A people without the knowledge of their past history, origin and culture is like a tree without roots.

- Marcus Garvey

273. Worry is a cycle of inefficient thoughts whirling around a center of fear.

- Corrie Ten Boom

274. It is better to risk saving a guilty man than to condemn an innocent one.

- Voltaire

275. Fortune is blind, but not invisible.

- French Proverb

276. Condemn none: if you can stretch out a helping hand, do so. If you cannot, fold your hands, bless your brothers, and let them go their own way.

- Swami Vivekananda

277. Dying is nothing. So start by living. It's less fun and it lasts longer.

– Romeo et Jeanette

278. The end of man is an action and not a
thought, though it were the noblest.

– Thomas Carlyle

279. Finite to fail, but infinite to venture.

- Emily Dickinson

280. A likely impossibility is always
preferable to an unconvincing possibility.

- Aristotle

281. There is no worse lie than a truth
misunderstood by those who hear it.

– William James

282. Doing the best at this moment puts you in
the best place for the next moment.

- Oprah Winfrey

283. The unhappy derive comfort from the
misfortune of others.

- Aesop

284. It has become appallingly obvious that
our technology has exceeded our humanity.

- Albert Einstein

285. I don't like that man. I must know him.

- Abraham Lincoln

286. Lies take more energy and yet they are easier and more common that the truth.

- J. Michael Straczynski

287. Successful people make money. It's not that people who make money become successful, but that successful people attract money. They bring success to what they do.

- Wayne Dyer

288. My fate cannot be mastered it can only be collaborated with and thereby, to some extent, directed. Nor am I the captain of my soul; I am only its noisiest passenger.

- Anon

289. Dependency is death to initiative, to risk-taking and opportunity. It's time to stop the spread of dependency and fight it like the poison it is.

- Mitt Romney

290. We have broken the cycle of dependency. People have found out they're better off working.

- John Engler

291. You can't choose up sides on a round world.

- Wayne Dyer

292. One is never as unhappy as one thinks,
nor as happy as one hopes.

– Dud de la Rochefoucauld

293. That's the great paradox of living on this
earth, that in the midst of great pain you can
have great joy as well. If we didn't have
those things we'd just be numb.

- Kathy Matthea

294. My great concern is not whether you
have failed, but whether you are content with
your failure.

- Abraham Lincoln

295. He that is discontented in one place will
seldom be happy in another.

- Aesop

296. The only thing worse than your heart
breaking is your heart hardening.

- Anon

297. The fact that you can love something that
you've lost is all the incentive you need to
love again, as opposed to becoming
comfortably numb.

- Cee Lo Green

298. One man that has a mind and knows it can always beat ten men who haven't and don't.

 – George Bernard Shaw

299. Saying nothing sometimes says the most.

- Emily Dickinson

300. As far as we can discern, the sole purpose of human existence is to kindle a light of meaning in the darkness of mere being.

 – C.G. Jung
(Memories, Dreams, Reflection)

301. All good books have one thing in common – they are truer than if they had really happened.

- Ernest Hemingway

302. If life were predictable, it would cease to be life, and be without flavor.

- Eleanor Roosevelt

303. Few people are capable of expressing with equanimity opinions which differ from the prejudices of their social environment. Most people are even incapable of forming such opinions.

- Albert Einstein

304. Success is counted sweetest by those who
     never succeed.

                              - Emily Dickinson

305. We were created to create ourselves.

                              - Anon

306. You can never really live anyone else's
     life, not even your child's. The influence you
     exert is through your own life, and what
     you've become yourself.

                              - Eleanor Roosevelt

307. It is more shameful to distrust our friends
     than to be deceived by them.

                              - Confucius

308. To see the right and not to do it is
     cowardice.

                              - Kong Qiu

309. Ability will never catch up with the
     demand for it.

                              - Chinese Proverb

310. Free will and destiny are two different
     paths that will hopefully meet each other at
     the end of a long road.

                              - Anon

311. Coincidence is the word we use when we can't see the levers and pulleys.

– Emma Bull

312. Most cancer-related deaths can be prevented through simple and painless preventive measures. A late diagnosis can result in more serious, long-term consequences.

- Olympia Snowe

313. The power of intuitive understanding will protect you from harm.

- Lao Tzu

314. Friends are like fiddle strings, they must not be screwed too tight.

- English Proverb

315. I wonder if Americans aren't fooled by our accent into detecting brilliance that may not really be there.

- Stephen Fry

316. Friends are lost by calling often and calling seldom.

- French Proverb

317. Friendship is a furrow in the sand.

- Tongan Proverb

318. Give no counsel till you are asked for it.
                                    - Italian Proverb

319. I learned to change my accent; in
England, your accent identifies you very
strongly with a class, and I did not want to be
held back.

                                              - Sting

320. Look at the means which a man employs,
consider his motives, observe his pleasures.
A man simply cannot conceal himself.
                                          - Confucius

321. A man's errors are his portals of
discovery.

                                      - James Joyce

322. Just because a path isn't well lit does not
mean it cannot be walked on.
                                           - Anon

323. Two things motivate people to achieve
success: inspiration and desperation.
                                           - Anon

324. You can have all the facts and be wrong.
                                           - Anon

325. If I shall exist eternally, how shall I exist tomorrow?

- Franz Kafka

326. Discovery consists of seeing what everybody has seen and thinking what nobody has thought.

– Albert von Szent-Gyorgyi

327. As you get older it is harder to have heroes, but it is sort of necessary.

- Ernest Hemingway

328. A great empire, like a great cake, is most easily diminished at the edges.

- Benjamin Franklin

329. Mediocre minds usually dismiss anything which reaches beyond their own understanding.

- Francoise de La Rochefoucauld

330. It is better to be the hammer than the anvil.

- Emily Dickinson

331. You shouldn't believe everything you hear but you should also not dismiss everything you hear.

- Anon

332. God hangs the greatest weights upon the smallest wires.

> - Francis Bacon

333. He that will not apply new remedies must expect new evils; for time is the greatest innovator.

> - Francis Bacon

334. If matters of truth and justice, there is no difference between large and small problems, for issues concerning the treatment of people are all the same.

> - Albert Einstein

335. If people have split views about your work, I think it's flattering. I'd rather have them feel something about it than dismiss it.

> - Stephen Sondheim

336. The value of a man should be seen in what he gives and not in what he is able to receive.

> - Albert Einstein

337. Have a horse of your own and then you may borrow another's.

> - Welsh Proverb

338. Glutton: one who digs his grave with his teeth.

- French Proverb

339. I know not with what weapons World War III will be fought, but World War IV will be fought with sticks and stones.

- Albert Einstein

340. Concealing an illness is like keeping a beach ball under water.

- Karen Duffy

341. God gives the nuts, but he doesn't crack them.

- German Proverb

342. The secret of learning to be sick is this: Illness doesn't make you less of what you were. You are still you.

- Tony Snow

343. Acclaim is a distraction.

- James Broughton

344. Half a loaf is better than a full loaf tomorrow.

- Anon

345. Art is the fatal net which catches these strange moments on the wing like mysterious butterflies, fleeing the innocence and distraction of common men.

- Giorgio de Chirico

346. Go to the door that's open, not the one that's closed.

- Anon

347. A casual stroll through the lunatic asylums shows that faith does not prove anything.

- Friedrich William Nietzsche

348. It is forbidden to kill: therefore all murders are punished unless they kill in large numbers and to the sound of trumpets.

- Voltaire

349. He is not wise that is not wise for himself.

- English Proverb

350. Not enough is better than nothing.

- Anon

351. He that lives on hope will die fasting.

352. Don't see the truth, be the truth.

- Franz Kafka

353. Don't cheat anyone, not even the world.

- Franz Kafka

354. Every man carries two bags about with him, one in front and one behind, and both are packed full of faults. The bag in front contains his neighbors faults, the one behind his own. Hence it is that men do not see their own faults, but never fail to see those of others.

- Aesop

355. Idleness is the beginning of all vice, the crown of all virtues.

- Franz Kafka

356. He makes his home where living is best.

- Latin Proverb

357. He that can't endure the bad will not live to see the good.

- Jewish Proverb

358. He that is of the opinion money will do everything may well be suspected of doing

everything for money.
> \- Benjamin Franklin

359. The cosmos is a gigantic flywheel,
      making 10,000 revolutions a minute. Man is
      a sick fly taking a dizzy ride on it. Religion is
      the theory that the wheel was designed and
      set spinning to give him the ride.
> – H. L. Mencken

360. Fortune befriends the bold.
> \- Emily Dickinson

361. Gossip is called gossip because it's not
      always the truth.
> \- Justin Timberlake

362. Serenity isn't boredom. Drama addiction
      is.
> \- Anon

363. When you hear hooves, don't expect a
      zebra.
> \- Anon

364. Our last thoughts before we sleep follow
      us into our slumber. Make the most of your
      last thoughts.
> – Lisa Nichols

365. There is a place where dreams survive.

– Stan Bush

366. Always do sober what you said you would do drunk. That will teach ya.

– Ernest Hemingway

367. We drink to drown our sorrows, but sorrows swim.

- Anon

368. Drinking your problems away is like using an anesthetic on a wound. It numbs the pain, but you still need to treat the problem.

- Anon

369. We cannot be blameless in our drunken actions, because we chose to put the first drink in our bodies.

- Anon

370. What is said while drunk has been thought beforehand.

- Anon

371. You choose to drink, so you can choose to stop.

- Anon

372. Nobody wakes up and is suddenly an

alcoholic.

- Anon

373. As long as habit and routine dictate the pattern of living, new dimensions of the soul will not emerge.

- Henry Van Dyke

374. Never trust a brilliant idea until it survives the hangover.

- Ernest Hemingway

375. When you're finished changing, you're finished.

- Benjamin Franklin

376. A great pretend is a fragile construct.

- Anon

377. What's a sundial in the shade?

- Benjamin Franklin

378. Without the element of uncertainty, the bringing off of even the greatest triumph would be dull, routine and eminently unsatisfying.

- J. Paul Getty

379. Time is money.

- Benjamin Franklin

380. The finest warrior hardly needs to know how to construct a rifle or understand the chemistry of gunpowder

- Anon

381. If you are happy, you don't need drugs. If you're not, then they aren't going to help.

- Anon

382. Drugs are a bet with your mind.

- Jim Morrison

383. Read not to contradict and confute, nor to believe and take for granted... but to weigh and consider.

- Francis Bacon

384. It takes as much energy to wish as it does to plan.

- Eleanor Roosevelt

385. All stories, if continued far enough, end in death, and he is no true-story teller who would keep that from you.

- Ernest Hemingway

386. The man who is always talking about being a gentleman never is one.

- R.S. Surtees

387. Friendship increases not in visiting
   friends, but in visiting them seldom.

> \- Francis Bacon

388. A penny saved is a penny earned.

> \- Benjamin Franklin

389. Write your injuries in dust, your benefits
   in marble.

> \- Benjamin Franklin

390. To live is so startling, it leaves time for
   little else.

> \- Emily Dickinson

391. No one is cockier than one who's bad at
   what he does.

> \- Anon

392. Talking about oneself is a means of
   concealing one's insecurities.

> \- Anon

393. We only brag about what we know won't
   last.

> \- Anon

394. Opportunity makes a thief.

> \- Francis Bacon

395. A fool always finds a greater fool who admires him, and flatterers live at the expense of the listeners.

- Anon

396. As soon as you say you got what you wanted, you lose it—success, ambition, drive. The claiming of it makes it disappear.

- Anon

397. When dealing with people, remember you are not dealing with creatures of logic but creatures of emotion.

- Dale Carnegie

398. Goals must never be from your ego, but problems that cry for a solution.

- Robert H. Schuller

399. Emotion can be a straightjacket.

- Anon

400. Emotion, like all fragile things, must be handled with care.

- Anon

401. A disembodied emotion is a non-existent one.

– Theodule Ribot

402. He that maketh haste to be rich shall not
be innocent.

> - Bible – Proverbs 28:20

403. When you start to develop your powers
of empathy and imagination, the whole world
opens up to you.

> - Susan Sarandon

404. He that plants thorns must never expect
to gather roses.

> - English Proverb

405. Suffering is only intolerable when
nobody cares.

> - Cicely Saunders

406. Offers sound so appealing if they involve
running away.

> - Anon

407. The eternal mystery of the world is its
comprehensibility...the fact that it is
comprehensible is a miracle.

> – Albert Einstein

408. Punctuated Equilibrium – We are not
guaranteed Earth. We must earn this world.

> – Stephen Jay Gould

409. Justice cannot be for one side alone, but must be for both.

> - Eleanor Roosevelt

410. Neither by nature, then, nor contrary to nature do the virtues arise in us; nature gives us the capacity to receive them, and this capacity is brought to maturity by habit.

> – Aristotle

411. When we try to escape from our mistakes, we actually tend to run toward them.

> - Anon

412. If we don't empower ourselves with knowledge, then we're gonna be led down a garden path.

> - Fran Drescher

413. The same sun and moon shine on us no matter where we are in the world.

> - Anon

414. Don't go somewhere that's got no answers.

> - Anon

415. He that seeks trouble never misses.

- English Proverb

416. To enter into your own mind, you need to be armed to the teeth.

– Paul Valery

417. As soon as men decide that all means are permitted to fight an evil, then their good becomes indistinguishable from the evil that they set out to destroy.

– Christopher Dawson

418. A belief in a supernatural source of evil is not necessary; mankind alone is quite capable of every wickedness imaginable.

- Anon

419. When life is too easy for us, we must beware or we may not be ready to meet the blows which sooner or later come to everyone, rich or poor.

- Eleanor Roosevelt

420. There is scarcely a single man sufficiently aware to know all the evil he does.

- Duc de la Rochefoucauld

421. It is .0000001 percent of the people who make 99.9999 percent of the important decisions of the world.

- Alan Moore

422. There are no necessary evils, only weak compromises.

- Anon

423. Man is neither good or bad; he is born with instinct and abilities.

– Honore de Balzac

424. If all pulled in one direction, the world would keel over.

- Yiddish Proverb

425. He who asks is a fool for five minutes, but he who does not ask remains a fool forever.

- Chinese Proverb

426. If the patient dies, the doctor has killed him, but if he gets well, the saints have saved him.

- Italian Proverb

427. An exaggeration is a truth that has lost its temper.

– Kahil Gibran

428. He who cannot agree with his enemies is controlled by them.

429. We can exaggerate our failures to justify them.

> - Anon

430. Exaggeration is a blood relation to falsehood and nearly as blameable.

> - Hosea Ballou

431. Nothing is absolute, with the debatable exceptions of this statement and death.

> - John Ralston Saul

432. Several excuses are always less convincing than one.

> – Aldous Huxley

433. If you are good at making excuses, you are rarely good at anything else.

> - Anon

434. If two men ride a horse, one must ride behind.

> - Anon

435. If you believe the doctors, nothing is wholesome; if you believe the theologians, nothing is innocent; if you believe the soldiers, nothing is safe.

436. Empty souls tend to extreme opinions.
                          - William Butler Yeats

437. Extremes, though contrary, have the like effects. Extreme heat kills, and so extreme cold: extreme love breeds satiety, and so extreme hatred; and too violent rigor tempts chastity, as does too much license.
                          - George Chapman

438. Logical consequences are the scarecrows of fools and the beacons of wise men.
                          – T.H. Huxley.

439. Just because a million people believe in a dumb idea, that doesn't change the fact that it's a dumb idea.
                          - Anon

440. The deepest sin against the human mind is to believe things without evidence.
                          – T.H. Huxley

441. It takes many good deeds to build a reputation and only one to lose it.
                          - Benjamin Franklin

442. Unforgiveness prolongs past mistakes.

443. Good fame is like fire; when you have kindled you may easily preserve it; but if you extinguish it, you will not easily kindle it again.

- Francis Bacon

444. Those who cheer today may hurl stones tomorrow.

- Anon

445. If you are planning for a year, sow rice; if you are planning for a decade, plant trees; if you are planning for a lifetime, educate people.

- Chinese Proverb

446. Happy families are all alike; every unhappy family is unhappy in its own way.

– Leo Tolstoy

447. It's easier to resist at the beginning than at the end.

- Leonardo da Vinci

448. It is well, when judging a friend, to remember that he is judging you with the same godlike and superior impartiality.

- Arnold Bennett

449. Once the toothpaste is out of the tube, it's awfully hard to get it back in.

- Anon

450. It is easier to forgive an enemy than to forgive a friend.

– William Blake

451. In a calm sea, every man is a pilot.

- Spanish Proverb

452. If you believe everything you read, better not read.

- Japanese Proverb

453. In baiting a mousetrap with cheese, always leave room for the mouse.

- Greek Proverb

454. To appreciate heaven, it's good for a person to have some 15 minutes of hell.

- Will Carleton

455. It is a bold mouse that nestles in the cat's ear.

- English Proverb

456. God must love the common man, he made so many of them.

- Abraham Lincoln

457. God does not play dice.

- Albert Einstein

458. 'Did you gut the pillow with a knife?'
What were the results?'
'Feathers,' she said. Feathers; everywhere,
Father.' '
Now I want you to go back and gather up
every last feather,'
'Well,' she said, 'it can't be done. The wind
took them all over.'
'And that,' said Father O' Rourke, 'is gossip!'
- Father Brendan Flynn
(Doubt)

459. Gossip: humanity's most pointless sin. It
tends to be the origin of all others.

- Anon

460. Most rumors start by remembering the
past wrong.

- Anon

461. In matters of truth and justice, there is no
difference between large and small problems,
for issues concerning the treatment of people
are all the same.

- Albert Einstein

462. People always whip themselves into a gossiping frenzy of misinformed speculation.

- Anon

463. Bullying in school used to be name-calling or physical abuse. Now people just spread spiteful rumors.

- Anon

464. There's more power in rumors than in truth. A fact can be disproven, but a rumor lingers forever.

- Anon

465. Remember, the only thing that gets thicker when spread is rumor.

- Anon

466. Nothing is so firmly believed as that which we least know.

– Montaigne

467. Grief for the dead is mad; it is an injury to the living, and the dead know it not.

- Xenophon

468. How many legs does a dog have if you call the tail a leg? Four. Calling a tail a leg doesn't make it a leg.

- Abraham Lincoln

469. A death isn't like losing a job or getting a divorce. There is no "getting over it." You have to integrate it into your life and live with it. It isn't like stopping a bomb going off. It is the bomb going off, and you have to survive somehow.

- Anon

470. Slow but steady wins the race.

- Aesop

471. Outside show is a poor substitute for inner worth.

- Aesop

472. He who joyfully marches to music in rank and file has already earned my contempt. He has been given a large brain by mistake, since for him the spinal cord would suffice.

- Albert Einstein

473. Given a choice between grief and nothing, I'd choose grief.

- William Faulkner

474. Men are nearly always willing to believe what they wish.

– Julius Caesar

475. It is a long road that has no turning.
- Irish Proverb

476. To his dog, every man is Napoleon;
hence the constant popularity of dogs.
- Aldous Huxley

477. Many forms of Government have been
tried and will be in this world of sin and woe.
No one pretends that democracy is perfect or
all-wise. Indeed, it has been said that
democracy is the worst form of government
except all those other forms that have been
tried from time to time.
- Winston Churchill

478. All gods are homemade, and it is we who
pull their strings, and so, give them the
power to pull ours.
- Aldous Huxley

479. It is easier to prevent bad habits than to
break them.
- Benjamin Franklin

480. Those that can make you believe in
absurdities can make you commit atrocities.
- Voltaire

481. Gradually changing habits makes more
      difference than changing them all at once.
                                    - Ian K. Smith

482. Success is to be measured not so much by
      the position that one has reached in life as by
      the obstacles which he has overcome.
                              - Booker T. Washington

483. Our suggestibility knows no limits.
                                    – David Mamet

484. It's not that I'm so smart, it's just that I
      stay with problems longer.
                                    - Albert Einstein

485. I never see what has been done; I only
      see what remains to be done.
                                    - Buddha

486. I am indebted to my father for living, but
      to my teacher for living well.
                              - Alexander the Great

487. Nothing ever comes to one, that is worth
      having, except as a result of hard work.
                              - Booker T. Washington

488. Remember not only to say the right thing in the right place, but far more difficult still, to leave unsaid the wrong thing at the tempting moment.

- Benjamin Franklin

489. The best way to get a bad law repealed is to enforce it strictly.

- Abraham Lincoln

490. It is thrifty to prepare today for the wants of tomorrow.

- Aesop

491. We all like to hide behind hard work, but hard work doesn't guarantee results.

- Steve Woodward

492. Love, friendship, respect do not unite people as much as common hatred for something.

– Anton Chekhov

493. Men often applaud an imitation and hiss the real thing.

- Aesop

494. No one is born hating. People must learn to hate.

- Nelson Mandela

495. Is the pious loved by the gods because it is pious, or is it pious because they love it?
- Plato

496. Virtue is persecuted more by the wicked than it is loved by the good.
- Buddha

497. No morality can be founded on authority, even if the authority were divine.
- A.J. Ayer

498. Heaven cannot brook two suns, nor earth two masters.
- Alexander the Great

499. Success in life is founded upon attention to the small things rather than to the large things; to the everyday things nearest to us rather than to the things that are remote and uncommon.
- Booker T. Washington

500. Psychoanalysis is a technique to cure excessively suffering individuals of the unconsciously misdirected desires that weave around their private webs of unreal terror and ambivalent attractions.

- Joseph Campbell

501. It is not enough to run, one must start in time.

- French Proverb

502. It is not the horse that draws the cart, but the oats.

- Russian Proverb

503. I shall allow no man to belittle my soul by making me hate him.

- Booker T. Washington

504. Know your limitations. Never accept them.

- Anon

505. There are two ways of exerting one's strength; one is pushing down, the other is pulling up.

- Booker T. Washington

506. Not all who hesitate are lost. The psyche has many secrets in reserve. And these are not disclosed unless required.

- Joseph Campbell

507. It is an equal failing to trust everybody and to trust nobody.

508. It is hard to pay for bread that has been eaten.
- Danish Proverb

509. It's so easy to manipulate, but it's nearly always clear that you are being manipulated.
- John Boorman

510. It is better to be born a beggar than a fool.
- Spanish Proverb

511. Hypocrisy is the outside of cynicism.
- Mason Cooley

512. It is better to conceal one's knowledge than to reveal one's ignorance.
- Spanish Proverb

513. Fate is the word cowards use to describe the things we are too weak to change.
- Friedrich Nietzsche

514. It is sweet to drink but bitter to pay for.
- Irish Proverb

515. Life is a foreign language all men mispronounce.

- Christopher Morley

516. Keep a thing for seven years and you'll find a use for it.

- Irish Proverb

517. When elephants fight, it is the ground that suffers.

- Anon

518. Every man who knows how to read has it in his power to magnify himself, to multiply the ways in which he exists, to make his life full, significant and interesting.

- Aldous Huxley

519. No greater injury can be done to any youth than to let him feel that because he belongs to this or that race, he will be advanced in life regardless of his own merits or efforts.

- Booker T. Washington

520. Man goes into the noisy crowd to drown his own clamor of silence.

- Radindranath Tagore

521. The difference between stupidity and genius is that genius has its limits.

- Albert Einstein

522. If you hate a person, you hate something in him that is part of yourself. What isn't part of ourselves doesn't disturb us.

– Hermann Hesse

523. Like a lame man's legs that hang limp is a proverb in the mouth of a fool.

- Bible – Proverbs 26:7

524. Kill not the goose that lays the golden egg.

- English Proverb

525. The quarrel of friends are the opportunities of foes.

- Anon

526. Life is a bridge. Cross over it, but build no house on it.

- Indian Proverb

527. Life without a friend is death without a witness.

- Spanish Proverb

528. He who wishes to fight must first count the cost.

- Sun Tzu
(The Art of War)

529. If the actual victory is long and far, you will exhaust your strength if you face it head on.

> \- Sun Tzu
> (The Art of War)

530. Hell isn't merely paved with good intentions; it's walled and roofed with them. Yes, and furnished too.

> \- Aldous Huxley

531. Cleverness has never been associated with long delays.

> \- Anon

532. If you do what you always do, you get what you always get.

> \- Anon

533. The magic of first love is our ignorance that it can't ever end.

> \- Benjamin Disraeli

534. Hunger is the best cook.

> \- Italian Proverb

535. I don't believe in depriving myself of any food or being imprisoned by a diet.

> \- Joely Fisher

536.	The trouble with always trying to preserve the health of the body is that it is so difficult to do without destroying the health of the mind.

- Gilbert K. Chesterton

537.	To a hungry man, there is no bad bread.
- French Proverb

538.	Oat bread today is better than cake tomorrow.
- Yugoslavian Proverb

539.	The radical of one century is the conservative of the next.

- Anon

540.	Listen to the sound of a river and you will get a trout.
- Irish Proverb

541.	Many would die before they think. And they do.
- Bertrand Russell

542.	Live with wolves, and you learn to howl.
- Spanish Proverb

543.	Never cut what can be united.

544. Mankind is divisible into two great classes; hosts and guests.

— Max Beerbohm
(And Even Now)

545. The will to be or become has been replaced by the will to seem.

- Alfred Adler

546. Men count up the faults of those who keep them waiting.

- French Proverb

547. False face must hide what the false heart doth know.

— William Shakespeare

548. Mere words do not feed the friars.

- Irish Proverb

549. A strong sense of identity gives man an idea he can do no wrong; too little accomplishes the same.

- Djuna Barnes

550. How frightful is man's condition! There is not one of his joys which does not come from some ignorance or other.

- Honor de Balzac

551. Point me out the happy man and I will
point you out either egotism, selfishness evil
– or else absolute ignorance.
– Graham Greene

552. We are all ill-equipped to comprehend
the very small and very large.
– Richard Dawkins

553. More grows in the garden than the
gardener knows he has sown.
- Spanish Proverb

554. Whenever two people meet, there are
really six people, there is each man as he sees
himself, each man as the other sees him, and
each man as he really is.
– William James

555. No man limps because another is hurt.
- Danish Proverb

556. Propaganda does not deceive people; it
merely helps them to deceive themselves.
- Eric Hoffer

557. No rose is without a thorn or a love
without a rival.

- Turkish Proverb

558. One father is more than a hundred
schoolmasters.

- English Proverb

559. Much reading is an oppression of the
mind, and extinguishes the natural candle,
which is the reason of so many senseless
scholars in the world.

- William Penn
(Fruits of a Father's Love)

560. To live in fear is to not live at all.

- Anon

561. One should look long and carefully at
oneself before one considers judging others.

- Moliere

562. We may often be of more consequence in
our own eyes than in the eyes of others.

- Anon

563. Man differs from other animals in that he
is the most imitative of creatures, and he
learns his earliest lessons by imitation.
Inborn in all of us is this instinct.

– Aristotle

564. Winning is a habit. So is losing.

- Vince Lombardi

565. Giving a phenomenon a label does not explain it.

- Taylor Caldwell

566. Mimicry is the most common form of flattery but it is not your own.

- Anon

567. The scientific approach to the phenomenon of human nature enables us to be ignorant without being frightened and without therefore having to invent all sorts of weird theories to explain away all the gaps in knowledge.

– D. W. Winnicott

568. It's more fun to arrive to a conclusion than to justify it.

- Malcolm Forbes

569. Blame is just a lazy way for a person to make sense of chaos.

- Doug Coupland

570. Immortal mortals and mortal immortals, living the others death and dying the other's life.

– Herodotus

571. Death cancels everything but truth, and strips a man of everything but genius and virtue. It is a sort of natural canonization.
                                                    - William Hazlitt

572. No one means all he says, and yet very few say all they mean, for words are slippery and thought is viscous.
                                                    – Henry Brooks Adams

573. One flower will not make a garland.
                                                    - French Proverb

574. It is commonly said that the most powerful weapon is the truth, but I think it can be the twisting of truths.
                                                    - Anon

575. A lie is the only substitute for the truth. It's not a great one, but it's the only one known and seems to be used just as often.
                                                    - Anon

576. Three things cannot be long hidden: the sun, the moon, and the truth.
                                                    - Buddha

577. All that is buried is not dead.
                                                    - Olive Schreiner

578. No mistake is more common and more fatuous than appealing to logic in cases which are beyond her jurisdiction.

- Samuel Butler

579. The universe is not only queerer than we suppose but queerer than we can suppose.

– J.B.S. Halone.

580. Love is like heaven but can hurt like hell.

- Anon

581. The heart has its reason that reason cannot answer.

- Anon

582. Your perfect love is rarely convenient love.

- Anon

583. For we do not easily expect evil of those whom we love most.

– Peter Abelard

584. What the mass media offers is not popular art, but entertainment which is intended to be consumed like food, forgotten, and replaced by a new dish.

- W. H. Auden

585. Media exist to invest our lives with
      artificial perceptions and arbitrary values.
                              - Marshall McLuhan

586. The mask if worn long enough will be the
      face.
                                 - Stephen Fry

587. One generation plants the trees; another
      gets the shade.
                              - Chinese Proverb

588. Behind every face, the mental emptiness
      deepen.
                                 - T.S. Elliott

589. One joy scatters a thousand griefs.
                              - Chinese Proverb

590. Home is the place, where when you have
      to go there, they have to take you in.
                                 - Robert Frost

591. Example is not the main thing in
      influencing others, it is the only thing.
                              - Albert Schweitzer

592. A lack of money is the root of all evil.

593. I mean there is something sort of
      insincere about changing your nose. If that's
      all that makes or breaks you, the shape of a
      piece of cartilage? I mean if you're going to
      go through life building everything on that?
      – Felice
(After The Fall)

594. If it has to choose who is to be crucified,
      the crowd will always save Barabbas.
      – Jean Cocteau
(Le Rappel a l'ordre)

595. One should go invited to a friend in good
      fortune, and uninvited in misfortune.
      - Swedish Proverb

596. Life is like the children's game of Snakes
      and Ladders—except there are a lot more
      snakes and they drop you farther down.
      - Anon

597. At least I have the modesty to admit that
      lack of modesty is one of my failings.
      - Hector Berlioz

598. Comedy is tragedy that happens to other
      people.

– Angela Carter

599. Nothing helps a bad mood like spreading it around.

- Bill Watterson

600. The New Age? Ha! It's just the old age stuck in a microwave oven for fifteen seconds.

- James Randi

601. Only the wearer knows where the shoe pinches.

- English Proverb

602. Ridicule is the only weapon to unintelligent propositions.

- Richard Dawkins

603. There are only two classes of pedestrians in these days of reckless motor traffic – the quick and the dead.

– James Dewar

604. The hottest place in Hell is reserved for those who remain neutral in times of great moral conflict.

- Martin Luther King Jr

605. Put silk on a goat, and it's still a goat.

606. If you are neutral in situations of injustice, you have chosen the side of the oppressor. If an elephant has its foot on the tail of a mouse and you say that you are neutral, the mouse will not appreciate the neutrality.

- Desmond Tutu

607. We live in a universe in which there are laws, just as there is a law of gravity. If you fall off a building it doesn't matter if you're a good person or a bad person, you're going to hit the ground.

- Michael Bernard Beckwith

608. Innocence always calls mutely for protection, when we would be so much wiser to guard ourselves against it.

– Graham Greene

609. Innocence is like a leper who has lost his bell, wandering the world meaning no harm.

– Graham Greene

610. The past is foreign country. They do things differently there.

—L. Hartley

611. Dreams are always set in the past.

—A. Phillips

612. Memory is deceptive. It is colored by
today's events.

—Albert Einstein

613. Youth is vivid rather than happy, but
memory always remember the happy things.

- Bernard Lovell

614. The present is an age of talkers, and not
of doers, and the reason is, that the world is
growing old. We are so far advanced in the
Arts and Sciences, that we live in retrospect,
and dote on past achievement.

- William Hazlitt

615. Nostalgia is a self-defense mechanism to
cast our minds back to a more relaxing time
that probably never existed.

- Anon

616. He who rides a tiger is afraid to
dismount.

- Chinese Proverb

617. If one were to order all mankind to
choose the best set rules in the world, each
group would, after due consideration, regard
its own as being by far the best.

– George Herbert

618. Fear is the thought of admitted inferiority.

-Elbert Hubbard

619. Rain beats a leopard's skin, but it does not wash off the spots.

- Ashanti Proverb

620. A wrong concept misleads the understanding; a wrong deed degrades the whole man, and may eventually demolish the structure of the human ego.

- Muhammed Iqbal

621. Fear is pain arising from the anticipation of evil.

- Aristotle

622. You know you've got paranoia when you can't think of anything that's your fault.

- Robert M. Hutchins

623. Your pain is the breaking of the shell that encloses your understanding.

- Khalil Gibran

624. To him is in fear, everything rustles.

- Sophocles

625. If we scare ourselves with the nonexistent, we stand no chance facing real danger.

- Anon

626. The mind will always rebel at a direct command – go to sleep, fall in love, stop crying, don't get angry, say you're sorry, take back what you said, you don't have the guts to do that, listen, stop talking, relax, be quiet, wake up.

– David Mamet

627. The first half of our lives is ruined by our parents; the second half by our children.

- Anon

628. We tend to perfume and reinterpret; meanwhile imagining that all the flies in the ointment, all the hairs in the soup, are the faults of some unpleasant someone else.

- Joseph Campbell

629. A perfection of means, and confusion of aims, seems to be our main problem.

- Albert Einstein

630. A pedestal is as much a prison as any small, confined space.

- Gloria Steinem

631. I would do anything to be muscular
except exercise or eat right.

– Steve Martin

632. Those who think they have no time for
bodily exercise will sooner or later have to
find time for illness.

- Edward Stanley

633. Nearly all men can stand adversity, but if
you want to test a man's character, give him
power.

- Abraham Lincoln

634. Rats desert a sinking ship.

- French Proverb

635. What is the matter with the poor is
Poverty; what is the matter with the rich is
Uselessness.

- George Bernard Shaw

636. I'm not afraid of the darkness outside but
the darkness inside.

- Shelagh Delaney

637. It's not what's said that decides a
relationship but what's unsaid.

- Anon

638. The gods can only laugh when one prays
for money.

- Japanese Proverb

639. When Hitler attacked the Jews I was not
a Jew, therefore I was not concerned. And
when Hitler attacked Catholics, I was not a
Catholic, and therefore, I was not concerned.
And when Hitler attacked the unions and the
industrialists, I was not a member of the
unions and I was not concerned. Then, Hitler
attacked me and the Protestant church – and
there was nobody left to be concerned.

– Martin Niemoller

640. Intolerance of groups is often, strangely
enough, exhibited more strongly against
small differences than against fundamental
ones.

– Sigmund Freud

641. Work is only noticed when it's not done.

- Anon

642. We know what happens to people who
stay in the middle of the road. They get run
down.

– Aneurin Bevan

643. If people are good only because they fear punishment, and hope for reward, then we are a sorry lot indeed.

- Albert Einstein

644. It is human nature to instinctively rebel at obscurity or ordinariness.

- Taylor Caldwell

645. Give a man a fish and you will feed him for a day. Give him religion and he will starve to death praying for a fish.

- George Carlin

646. There's an invisible man living in the sky who watches everything you do. And the invisible man has a special list of ten things he does not want you to do. And if you do any of these ten things, he has a special place, full of fire and smoke and burning and torture and anguish, where he will send you to live and suffer and burn and choke and scream and cry forever and ever 'til the end of time!.....
But he loves you!

- George Carlin

647. He is poor indeed that can promise nothing.

- Thomas Fuller

648. Daughter am I in my mother's house but mistress in my own.

– Rupert Kipling

649. Since we cannot get what we like, let us like what we can get.

- Spanish Proverb

650. Habit and routine have an unbelievable power to waste and destroy.

- Henri de Lubac

651. Small children give you headache, big children heartache.

- Russian Proverb

652. I hate having my life disrupted by routine.

- Caskie Stinnett

653. In every aspect of life, there is a security blanket, a thumb to suck, a skirt to hold.

– Isaac Asimov

654. Just because something is comfortable doesn't mean it is right, safe, healthy, or real.

- Anon

655. Science is organized knowledge.

- Anon

656. We need pessimists as much as we need optimists. An optimist invented the airplane. A pessimist invented the parachute.

- Anon

657. Nothing fortifies skepticism more than the fact that there are some who are not skeptics; if all were so, they would be wrong.

- Blaise Pascal

658. A fool is a man who never tried an experiment in his life.

– Erasmus Darwin

659. A new scientific truth does not triumph by convincing its opponents and making them see the light, but rather because its opponents eventually die, and a new generation grows up that is familiar with it.

– Max Planck

660. Science is built up of facts, as a house is built of stones; but an accumulation of facts is no more a science than a heap of stones is a house.

- Henri Poincare

661. Science is not to open the door to infinite wisdom, but to set a limit to infinite error.

- Bertolt Brecht

662. Probable impossibilities are to be preferred to improbable possibilities.

- Aristotle

663. Truth exists; only lies are invented.

- Anon

664. They say the hardest part of a relationship is ending it but it isn't. That's the easiest part. All you have to do is stop trying. That's why nearly all of them end. The hardest part is keeping it.

- Aaron Chenowith

665. A desperate disease requires a dangerous remedy.

– Guy Fawkes

666. Fortunately, analysis is not the only way to resolve inner conflicts. Life itself still remains a very effective therapist.

- Karen Horney

667. Everyone suffers wrongs for which there is no remedy.

- Edgar Watson Howe

668. It is impossible for a man to organize his life with repressions.

– Arthur Miller

669. Some people are masters of money, and
      some its slaves.

      - Russian Proverb

670. Hateful to me as the gates of Hades is the
      man who hides one thing in his heart and
      says another.

      – Homer
      (The Iliad)

671. Sometimes I go about pitying myself, and
      all the time I am being carried on great wings
      across the sky.

      - Ojibway Saying

672. Your character is what you are, your
      reputation is what others think you are.

      - John Wooden

673. It is a revenge the devil sometimes takes
      upon the virtuous, that he entraps them by
      the force of the very passion they have
      suppressed and think themselves superior to.

      - George Santayana

674. Speak not of my debts unless you mean
      to pay them.

      - English Proverb

675. The road to a friend's house is never long.

- Danish Proverb

676. The tallest blade of grass is the first to be cut by the scythe.

- Russian Proverb

677. Never in the field of human conflict was so much owed by so many to so few. A medal glitters, but it also casts a shadow.

- Winston Churchill

678. Sweet is wine but sour is the payment.

- Irish Proverb

679. He that studieth revenge keepeth his own wounds green, which otherwise would heal and do well.

- John Milton

680. The gem cannot be polished without friction, nor man perfected without trials.

- Chinese Proverb

681. A man's true secrets are more secret to himself than to others.

- Paul Valery

682. An eye for an eye leaves everyone blind.

- Anon

683. The girl who can't dance says the band can't play.

- Yiddish Proverb

684. Three can keep a secret, if two of them are dead.

- Benjamin Franklin

685. Some do not choose, they settle. They go where they are pushed or pulled.

- Anon

686. If you look at life like rolling a dice, then my situation now, as it stands – yeah, it may only be a 3. If I jack that in now, go for something bigger and better, yeah, I could easily roll a 6 – no problem, I could roll a 6... I could also roll a 1.

– Tim
(The Office)

687. The tongue is to be feared more than the sword.

– Japanese Proverb

688. The tongue kills without drawing blood.

- Chinese Proverb

689. Facts do not cease to exist because they are ignored.

- Aldous Huxley

690. The wise adapt themselves to circumstances, as water molds itself to the pitcher.

- Chinese Proverb

691. The wise man sits on the hole in his carpet.

- Persian Proverb

692. Because I am a woman, I must make unusual efforts to succeed.
If I fail, no one will say, "She doesn't have what it takes."
They will say, "Women don't have what it takes.

— Clare Boothe Luce

693. The turtle lays thousands of eggs without anyone knowing, but when the hen lays an egg, the whole country is informed.

- Malay Proverb

694. The well-fed does not understand the lean.

- Irish Proverb

695. So long as men worship the Caesars and Napoleons, Caesars and Napoleons will duly arise and make them miserable.

- Aldous Huxley

696. Few things can help an individual more than to place responsibility on him, and to let him know that you trust him.

- Booker T. Washington

697. I am dying with the help of too many physicians.

- Alexander the Great

698. Dignity does not consist in possessing honors, but in deserving them.

- Aristotle

699. Important principles may, and must, be inflexible.

- Abraham Lincoln

700. The whisper of a pretty girl can be heard further than the roar of a lion.

- Arabian Proverb

701. Men often grudge others what they cannot enjoy themselves.

702. The Bible teaches us that woman brought sin and death into the world, which she precipitated the fall of the race...marriage for her was to be a condition of bondage, maternity a period of suffering and anguish, and in silence and subjection, she was to play the role of a dependent on man's bounty for all her material wants.
                              – Elizabeth Cady Stanton

703. The wolf loses his teeth, but not his inclinations.
                              - Spanish Proverb

704. If you can't sleep, then get up and do something instead of lying there worrying. It's the worry that gets you, not the lack of sleep.
                              - Dale Carnegie

705. I am not afraid of the lions led by the sheep. I am afraid of the sheep lead by the lions.
                              - Alexander the Great

706. Many a man is praised for his reserve and so-called shyness when he is simply to proud to risk making a fool of himself.

- J.B. Priestly

707. Some protect the here and now. Others protect the long-term invisible, unlikely, or non-existent.

- Anon

708. Foolish people do not understand that what is seen is merely their own mind.

- Mahayana Buddhist texts

709. Skilled or unskilled, we all scribble poems.

- Horace

710. I cannot and will not cut my conscience to fit this year's fashions.

– Lillian Hellman

711. The world would not make a racehorse of a donkey.

- Irish Proverb

712. A ruffled mind makes a restless pillow.

- Charlotte Bronte

713. There are many paths to the top of the mountain, but the view is always the same.

- Chinese Proverb

714. To deny all, is to confess all.

715. Course we're all gonna die someday. But do we have to pay for it? Do we have to actually throw hard-earned dollars down on the counter and say, "Please Mr. Merchant-of-Death, please, sell me something that'll stink up my breath and my clothes and fry my lungs.

- Chewies Gum Rep
(Clerks)

716. If we reduce social life to the smallest possible unit we will find that there is no social life in the company of one.

- Jerzy Kosinski

717. There is nothing to it. You only have to hit the right notes at the right time and the instrument plays itself.

– Johann Sebastian Bach

718. Though a tree grow ever so high, the falling leaves return to the ground.

- Malay Proverb

719. Particles, chaos, inertia, entropy. The universe doesn't give a damn.

- Anon

720. To teach is to learn.

- Japanese Proverb

721. You want to believe that there's one relationship in life that's beyond betrayal. A relationship that's beyond that kind of hurt. And there isn't.

- Caleb Carr

722. Eyes and ears are bad witnesses to men if they have souls that understand not their language.

- Anon

723. To talk without thinking is to shoot without aiming.

- English Proverb

724. The significance of man is that he is insignificant and is aware of it.

– Carl Becker

725. Nostalgia often leads to idle speculation.

- Paul Getty

726. Tomorrow is often the busiest day of the week.

- Spanish Proverb

727. The only thing worse than not changing is regressing.

- Anon

728. True nobility is in being superior to your previous self.

- Hindustani Proverb

729. There's nothing worse than having everybody thinking alike, talking alike and having the same direction in mind. It gets stale that way.

- Alex Van Halen

730. Trust in God but tie your camel.

- Muslim Proverb

731. All stories, if continued far enough, end in death, and he is no true-story teller who would keep that from you.

- Ernest Hemingway

732. Food can become such a point of anxiety - not because it's food, but just because you have anxiety. That's how eating disorders develop.

- Vanessa Carlton

733. As the rich consume more and more, they are clearly not going to want to downgrade their own status.

- Susan George

734. Some stories are true that never happened.

            - Elie Wiesel

735. Refusal to believe until proof is given is a rational position; denial of all outside of our own limited experience is absurd.

            - Annie Besant

736. Nothing can stress you out more than yourself.

            - Anon

737. To be ambitious for wealth, and yet always expecting to be poor; to be always doubting your ability to get what you long for, is like trying to reach east by travelling west. There is no philosophy which will help man to succeed when he is always doubting his ability to do so, and thus attracting failure.

            - Charles Baudouin

738. If you have abandoned one faith, do not abandon all faith. There is always an alternative. Or is the same faith under another mask?

            - Graham Greene

739. If you criticize something, then you have to have an alternative, but we do have to try and improve things.

- Linford Christie

740. The most distressing thing that can happen to a prophet is to be proved wrong. The next most distressing thing is to be proved right.

- Aldous Huxley

741. Ah, yes, superstition: it would appear to be cowardice in face of the supernatural.

- Anon

742. Truth and oil always come to the surface.

– Spanish Proverb

743. Our subconscious makes no dissimilarity between constructive and destructive thoughts. It takes what it is given.

- Tom Ryan

744. Truth has a handsome countenance but torn garments.

- German Proverb

745. Don't be superstitious. It will bring bad luck.

- Anon

746. Truth is the safest lie.

- Jewish Proverb

747. A bad book is as much of a labor to write as a good one, it comes as sincerely from the author's soul.

- Aldous Huxley

748. I count him braver who overcomes his desires than him who conquers his enemies; for the hardest victory is over self.

- Aristotle

749. The only way to keep your health is to eat what you don't want, drink what you don't like, and do what you'd rather not.

- Mark Twain

750. Education is an ornament in prosperity and a refuge in adversity.

- Aristotle

751. Two shorten the road.

- Irish Proverb

752. Opportunities may knock only once but temptation leans on the doorbell.

- Anon

753. Walk straight, my son – as the old crab said to the young crab.

- Irish Proverb

754. What you cannot avoid, welcome.

- Chinese Proverb

755. Superstition is rooted in the brain more deeply than skepticism.

– Johann Wolfgang von Goethe

756. What breaks in a moment may take years to mend.

- Swedish Proverb

757. It is a capital mistake to theorize before one has data. Insensibly one begins to twist facts to suit theories, instead of theories to suit facts.

- Sherlock Holmes
(A Scandal in Bohemia)

758. What one knows is sometimes useful to forget.

- Latin Proverb

759. Labor without joy is base. Labor without sorrow is base. Sorrow without labor is base.

- Anon

760. When a father helps a son, both smile;
but when a son must help his father, both cry.
- Jewish Proverb

761. If we could first know where we are, and
whither we are tending, we could then better
judge what to do, and how to do it.
- Abraham Lincoln

762. When you have got an elephant by the
hind legs and he is trying to run away, it's
best to let him run.
- Abraham Lincoln

763. In theory, there is no difference between
theory and practice, but in practice, there is.
- Anon

764. When ill luck falls asleep, let none wake
her.
- Italian Proverb

765. No written law has ever been more
binding than unwritten custom supported by
popular opinion.
– Carrie Chapman Catt

766. When spider webs unite, they can tie up a
lion.

- Ethiopian Proverb

767. When the mouse laughs at the cat, there is a hole nearby.

- Nigerian Proverb

768. When the apple is ripe, it will fall.

- Irish Proverb

769. When the sword of rebellion is drawn, the sheath should be thrown away.

- English Proverb

770. Tradition, long conditioned thinking, can bring about a fixation, a concept that one readily accepts, perhaps not with a great deal of thought.

- Jiddu Krishnamurti

771. To make an apple pie from scratch, you must first invent the universe.

- Albert Einstein

772. A common mistake that people make when trying to design something completely foolproof is to underestimate the ingenuity of complete fools.

- Douglas Adams

773. Nature abhors a vacuum.

774. Man is the only creature that consumes without producing.

- George Orwell

775. Every man is said to have his peculiar ambition. Whether is be true or not, I can say for one that I have no other so great as that of being truly esteemed of my fellow men, by rendering myself worthy of their esteem.

- Abraham Lincoln

776. The fact that we live at the bottom of a deep gravity well, on the surface of a gas covered planet going around a nuclear fireball ninety million miles away and think this is normal is some indication of how skewed our perspective tends to be.

- Douglas Adams

777. Yesterday is but a dream, tomorrow is but a vision. But today well lived makes every yesterday a dream of happiness, and every tomorrow a vision of hope. Look well, therefore, to This Day.

- Sanskrit Proverb

778. When you live next to the cemetery, you cannot weep for everyone.

779. You cannot reason with a hungry belly, it has no ears.

> - Greek Proverb

780. Beware that you do not lose the substance by grasping at the shadow.

> - Aesop

781. Any excuse will serve a tyrant.

> - Aesop

782. All men commend patience, although few are willing to practice it.

> - Thomas Kempis

783. Waiting is still an occupation. It's having nothing to wait for that is terrible.

> – Cesare Pavese

784. There is no greater pain than to remember a happy time when one is in misery.

> – Dante Alighieri

785. There is an eagle in me that wants to soar, and there is a hippopotamus in me that wants to wallow in the mud.

> - Carl Sandburg

786. We often give our enemies the means for our own destruction.

> \- Aesop

787. When your enemy falls, don't rejoice- but don't pick him up either.

> \- Yiddish Proverb

788. A lunatic cannot put out the sun by scribbling the word, 'darkness' on the walls of his cell.

> \- C. S. Lewis

789. Where the tongue slips, it speaks the truth.

> \- Irish Proverb

790. Who knows most, speaks least.

> \- Spanish Proverb

791. When we start deceiving ourselves into thinking not that we want something or need something, not that it is a pragmatic necessity for us to have it, but that it is a moral imperative that we have it, then is when we join the fashionable madmen, and then is when the thin whine of hysteria is heard in the land, and then we are in trouble.

> \- Joan Didion

792. Experience only teaches the teachable.
- Aldous Huxley

793. Never trust the advice of a man in difficulties.

- Aesop

794. It is a bit embarrassing to have been concerned with the human problem all one's life and find at the end that one has no more to offer by way of advice than "try to be a little kinder."
- Aldous Huxley

795. Solitude is painful when one is young, but delightful when one is more mature.
- Albert Einstein

796. The Rum Tum Tugger is a Curious Cat:
If you set him on a mouse then he only wants a rat,
If you set him on a rat then he'd rather chase a mouse.
-T.S. Eliot
(Old Possum's Book of Practical Cats)

797. It's easier to make war than to make peace.
– Georges Clemenceau

798. War is all that is offered in a world in desperate need of healing.

- Anon

799. You men may die, old men must.

- English Proverb

800. What forgets is the axe, but the tree that has been axed will never forget.

- Chinese Proverb

801. The opposite of war isn't peace; it's creation.

- Anon

802. A loose tooth will not rest until it's pulled out.

- Bulgarian Proverb

803. You can't end lives to save them.

- Anon

804. Measure thrice, cut once.

- Dutch Proverb

805. If you declare war on others, you declare war on yourself.

- Anon

806. If we knew what it was we were doing, it would not be called research, would it?
- Albert Einstein

807. Cynical realism is the intelligent man's best excuse for doing nothing in an intolerable situation.
- Aldous Huxley

808. Who is curious gets old quickly.
- Chinese Proverb

809. Reality is merely an illusion, albeit a very persistent one.
- Albert Einstein

810. The path is made by walking.
- Dutch Proverb

811. The way to win a war is to make certain it never starts.
- Omar Bradley

812. If the facts don't fit the theory, change the facts.
- Albert Einstein

813. Be a master of the mind, not mastered by the mind.

- Zen Proverb

814.   Alexander the Great....when he had conquered what was called the Eastern World...wept of more Worlds to conquer.
— Isaac Watts

815.   But if thought corrupts language, language can also corrupt thought.
- George Orwell

816.   All things can corrupt when minds are prone to evil.
- Ovid

817.   Time has no divisions to mark its passage; there is never a thunderstorm or blare of trumpets to announce the beginning of a new month. Even when a new century begins it is only we mortals who ring bells and fire off pistols.
- Thomas Mann

818.   There will always be a lost dog somewhere that will prevent me from being happy.
— La Sauvage
(The Restless Heart)

819.   Young wood makes a hot fire.

820. What's not destroyed by Time's
devouring hand? Where's Troy?"

– James Bramstom

821. The first law of dietetics seems to be if it
tastes good, it's bad for you.

– Isaac Asmiov

822. As we unweave a rainbow, it becomes
less wonderful.

– Richard Dawkins

823. Deeds are fruits, words are but leaves.

- Anon

824. Better to go back than go wrong.

- Buddhist Proverb

825. Distance lends enhancement to the view.

- Zen Proverb

826. Don't bargain for fish which are still in the
water.

- Indian Proverb

827. A king's child is a slave elsewhere.

- African Proverb

828. The only reason for time is so that everything doesn't happen at once.

                - Albert Einstein

829. Empty bags cannot stand upright.

                - Anon

830. Good company on the road is the shortest cut.

                - Budai

831. It is better to be green and growing than ripe and rotten.

                - Budai

832. The best ground bears weeds as well as flowers.

                - Zen Proverb

833. A chain is no stronger than its weakest link.

                - Anon

834. A short cut is often a wrong cut.

                - Anon

835. Little strokes fell great oaks.

                - Buddhist Proverb

836. Necessity is a hard nurse, but she raises strong children.

- English Proverb

837. Many drops make a shower.

- Anon

838. Lost time is never found again.

- Buddhist Proverb

839. A little body doth often harbor a great soul.

- Budai

840. A light purse makes a heavy heart.

- American Proverb

841. A little each day is much in a year.

- American Proverb

842. A man's intentions seldom add to his income.

- American Proverb

843. A poor man is better than a liar.

- English Proverb

844. A single penny fairly got is worth a thousand that are not.

- English Proverb

845. He who can no longer pause to wonder and stand rapt in awe, is as good as dead; his eyes are closed.

- Albert Einstein

846. Be happy while you are living for you are a long time dead.

- Scottish Proverb

847. Better to have than to wish.

- Anon

848. Advice when most needed is least heeded.

- Budai

849. We do not always gain by changing.

- Buddhist Proverb

850. The golden age never was the present one.

- Anon

851. If you don't know where you're going, then the journey is never ending.

- Zen Proverb

852. Hasty judgments are generally faulty.

- Buddhist Proverb

853. A close friend can become a close enemy.

- Ethiopian Proverb

854. No amount of experimentation can ever prove me right; a single experiment can prove me wrong.
> - Albert Einstein

855. The owl is the wisest of all birds, because the more it sees, the less it talks.
> - African Proverb

856. The fool wanders, the wise man travels.
> - Siddhartha Gautama

857. A courtyard common to all will be swept by none.
> - Chinese Proverb

858. A country can be judged by the quality of its proverbs.
> - German Proverb

859. A man is not old until his regrets take the place of his dreams.
> - Yiddish Proverb

860. A drowning man is not troubled by rain.
> - Persian Proverb

861. A friend's eye is a good mirror.

- Irish Proverb

862.Never before in history has innovation offered promise of so much to so many in so short a time.

- Bill Gates

863.A good husband is healthy and absent.

- Japanese Proverb

864.Logic is the beginning of wisdom, not the end.

- Leonard Nimoy

865.A wise man changes his mind, a fool never will.

- Spanish Proverb

866.A hedge between keeps friendship green.

- French Proverb

867.People always fear change. People feared electricity when it was invented, didn't they? People feared coal, they feared gas-powered engines… There will always be ignorance, and ignorance leads to fear.

- Bill Gates

868.He has enough who is content.

- Buddhist Proverb

869. From a certain point onward, there is no longer any turning back. That is the point that must be reached.

- Franz Kafka

870. Some people die at 25 and aren't buried until 75.

- Benjamin Franklin

871. I have no special talent. I am only passionately curious.

- Albert Einstein

872. Those that know, do. Those that understand, teach.

- Aristotle

873. I had rather excel others in the knowledge of what is excellent, than in the extent of my power and dominion.

- Alexander the Great

874. It is not necessary that you leave the house. Remain at your table and listen. Do not even listen, only wait. Do not even wait, be wholly still and alone. The world will present itself to you for its unmasking, it can do no other, in ecstasy it will writhe at your feet.

- Franz Kafka

875. The root of all superstition is that men observe when a thing hits, but not when it misses.

　　　　　　　　　　　　　- Francis Bacon

876. Hope is a good breakfast, but it is a bad supper.

　　　　　　　　　　　　　- Francis Bacon

877. Leave no stone unturned.

　　　　　　　　　　　　　- Euripides

878. He that can have patience can have what he will.

　　　　　　　　　　　　　- Benjamin Franklin

879. It's fine to celebrate success but it is more important to head the lessons of failure.

　　　　　　　　　　　　　- Bill Gates

880. Love is a better teacher than duty.

　　　　　　　　　　　　　- Albert Einstein

881. Nothing has more strength than dire necessity.

　　　　　　　　　　　　　- Euripides

882. A man can be destroyed but not defeated.

- Ernest Hemingway

883. It is not more vacation we need – it is more vocation.

- Eleanor Roosevelt

884. The mightiest ant will be crushed by the frailest of men.

- Anon

885. People need hard times and oppression to develop psychic muscles.

- Emily Dickinson

886. To love is so startling, it leaves little time for anything else.

- Emily Dickinson

887. Remember always that you not only have the right to be an individual, you have an obligation to be one.

- Eleanor Roosevelt

888. As for accomplishments, I just did what I had to do as things came along.

- Eleanor Roosevelt

889. You cannot open a book without learning.

- Confucius

890. The worst men often give the best advice.

- Francis Bacon

891. A gentleman would be ashamed should his deed not match his words.

        - Confucius

892. He that thinks himself the happiest man is really so; but he that thinks himself the wisest is generally the greatest fool.

        - Francis Bacon

893. Only the wisest and stupidest of men never change.

        - Kong Qiu

894. When anger rises, think of the consequences.

        - Kong Qiu

895. The superior man is distressed by the limitations of his ability; he is not distressed by the fact that men do not recognize the ability that he has.

        - Anon

896. The faults of a superior person are like the sun and moon. They have their faults, and everyone sees them; they change and everyone looks up to them.

        - Chinese Proverb

897. Truth is so rare that it is delightful to tell it.

- Emily Dickinson

898. When life is too easy for us, we must be aware or we may not be ready to meet the blows which sooner or later come to everyone.

- Eleanor Roosevelt

899. He that rises late must trot all day.

- Benjamin Franklin

900. Old age, believe me, is a good and pleasant thing. It is true you are gently shouldered off the stage, but then you are given such a comfortable front stall as spectator.

- Confucius

901. Wars are caused by undefended wealth.

- Ernest Hemingway

902. Association with human beings lures one into self-observation.

- Franz Kafka

903. There's no one thing that is true. They're all true.

- Ernest Hemingway

904. Houses are built to live in, and not to look on: therefore, let use be preferred before uniformity.

- Francis Bacon

905. There are three things extremely hard: steel, a diamond, and to know one's self.
- Benjamin Franklin

906. Wars are not paid for in wartime, the bill comes later.
- Anon

907. When in doubt, don't.
- American Proverb

908. He that displays too often his wife and his wallet is in danger of having both of them borrowed.
- English Proverb

909. The discontented man finds no easy chair.
- Benjamin Franklin

910. Young people are fitter to invent than to judge; fitter for execution than for counsel; and more fit for new projects than for settled business.
- Francis Bacon

911. Intellectuals solve problems, geniuses prevent them.
- Albert Einstein

912. We still do not know one thousandth of one percent of what nature has revealed to us.
- Albert Einstein

913. Who questions much shall learn much.
- Francis Bacon

914. I think that somehow, we learn who we really are and then live with that decision.
- Eleanor Roosevelt

915. In all our contacts, it is probably the sense of being really needed and wanted which gives us the greatest satisfaction and creates the most lasting bond.
- Anon

916. Even the loose cannon hits the target every once in a while.
- American Proverb

917. When will our conscience grow so tender that we will act to prevent human misery rather than avenge it?
- Anon

918. All mankind is divided into three classes: those that are immoveable, those that are moveable, and those that move.

- Benjamin Franklin

919. If we do not maintain justice, justice will not maintain us.

- Francis Bacon

920. Never do anything against conscience, even if the state demands it.

- Albert Einstein

921. Occurrences in this domain are beyond the reach of exact prediction because of the variety of factors in operation, not because of any lack of order in nature.

- Albert Einstein

922. I very rarely think in words at all. A thought comes, and I may try to express it in words afterwards.

- Albert Einstein

923. There is no logical way to the discovery of these elemental laws. There is only the way of intuition, which is helped by a feeling for order lying behind the appearance.

- Albert Einstein

924. A man wrapped up in himself makes a very small bundle.

- Benjamin Franklin

925. At twenty years of age, the will reigns; at thirty, the wit; and at forty, the judgment.

- Benjamin Franklin

926. If you desire many things, many things will seem few.

- Benjamin Franklin

927. Don't throw stones at your neighbors if your own windows are glass.

- Benjamin Franklin

928. Beware the hobby that eats.

- Benjamin Franklin

929. Nothing doth more hurt than that cunning men pass for wise.

- Francis Bacon

930. Truth is so hard to tell, it sometimes needs fiction to make it plausible.

- Francis Bacon

931. Riches are a good hand maiden but a poor mistress.

- Francis Bacon

932. Keep company with those who uplift you.

- Epictetus

933. Nothing is enough for the man to whom enough is too little.

- Epicurus

934. Death does not concern us, because as long as we exist, death is not here. And when it does come, we no longer exist.

- Epicurus

935. Not what we have but what we enjoy constitutes our abundance.

- Epicurus

936. It is not so much our friend's help that helps us, as the confidence of their help.

- Greek Proverb

937. The misfortune of the wise is better than the prosperity of the fool.

- Anon

938. The time when most of you should withdraw into yourself is when you are forced to be in a crowd.

- Greek Proverb

939. The gift of fantasy has meant more to me than my talent for absorbing positive knowledge.

- Albert Einstein

940. Give light and the darkness will disappear of
itself.

- Desiderius Erasmus

941. Prevention is better than cure.

- Desiderius Erasmus

942. I conceive that the great part of the miseries
of mankind are brought upon them by false
estimates they have made of the value of
things.

- Benjamin Franklin

943. The only thing that interferes with my
learning is my education.

- Albert Einstein

944. Fortune favors the audacious.

- Anon

945. There are some people who live in a dream
world, and there are some who face reality;
and then there are those who turn one into
the other.

- Desiderius Erasmus

946. Half a truth is often a great lie.

- Benjamin Franklin

947. Work as if you were to live a hundred years. Pray as if you were to die tomorrow.

- American Proverb

948. A countryman between two lawyers is like a fish between two cats.

- North American Proverb

949. It is a miracle that curiosity survives formal education.

- Albert Einstein

950. Joy in looking and comprehending is nature's most beautiful gift.

- Albert Einstein

951. Be careful to leave your sons well-instructed rather than rich, for the hopes of the instructed are better than the wealth of the ignorant.

- Epictetus

952. A nail is driven out by another nail. Habit is overcome by habit.

- Desiderius Erasmus

953. The attempt to combine wisdom and power has only rarely been successful and then only for a short while.

954. He who allows oppression shares the crime.

- Dutch Proverb

955. In the kingdom of the blind, the one-eyed man is king.

- Desiderius Erasmus

956. The desire to write grows with writing.

- Dutch Proverb

957. No one respects a talent that is concealed.

- Dutch Proverb

958. Fools are without number.

- Anon

959. When I get a little money, I buy a book; and if any is left, I buy food and clothes.

- Desiderius Erasmus

960. The devil has put a penalty on all things we enjoy in life. Either we suffer in health or we suffer in soul or we get fat.

- Albert Einstein

961. Most of the fundamental ideas of science are essentially simple, it may, as a rule, be expressed in a language comprehensible to everyone.

- Albert Einstein

962. Information is not knowledge.

- Albert Einstein

963. Confusion of goals and perfection seems to characterize our age.

- Anon

964. Small is the number of people who see with their eyes and think with their minds.

- Zen Proverb

965. Humility is truth.

- Desiderius Erasmus

966. To find joy in work is to discover the fountain of youth.

- Pearl S. Buck

967. I do not judge, I only chronicle.

- John Singer Sargent

968. Having been poor is no shame, but being ashamed of it, is.

- Benjamin Franklin

969. If you want to improve, be content to be thought foolish and stupid.

- Epictetus

970. Is freedom anything else than the right to live as we wish? Nothing else.

- Epictetus

971. Don't underestimate your opponent, but don't overestimate them, either.

- Nancy Pelosi

972. Do good to your friends to keep them, to your enemies to win them.

- Chinese Proverb

973. Only the educated are free.

- Greek Proverb

974. It is easier to prevent bad habits than to break them.

- American Proverb

975. We should not moor a ship with one anchor, or out life with one hope.

- Epictetus

976. Time takes away the grief of men.

- Desiderius Erasmus

977. It is only when the rich are sick that they fully feel the impotence of wealth.

- Benjamin Franklin

978. Whoever does not regard what he has as most ample wealth, he has as most ample wealth, is unhappy, though he be master of the world.

- Epictetus

979. Let every man be respected and no man idolized.

- Albert Einstein

980. What we need is more people who specialize in the impossible.

- Theodore Roethke

981. Have patience. All things are difficult before they become easy.

- Saadi

982. The more we elaborate our means of communication, the less we communicate.

- J.B. Priestley

983. People are not disturbed by things, but by the view they take of them.

- Epictetus

984. It is not folly to live in misery, it's human.

- Dutch Proverb

985. No great thing is created suddenly.

- Greek Proverb

986. Nowadays the rage for possession has got to such a pitch that there is nothing in the realm of nature, whether sacred or profane, out of which profit cannot be squeezed.

- Desiderius Erasmus

987. The most disadvantageous peace is better than the most just war.

- Desiderius Erasmus

988. Don't give your advice before you are called upon.

- Dutch Proverb

989. What difference is there, do you think, between those in Plato's cave who can only marvel at the shadows and images of various objects, provided they are content and don't know what they miss, and the philosopher who has emerged from the cave and sees the real things?

– Greek Proverb

990. A good portion of speaking will consist in knowing how to lie.

- Anon

991. War is sweet to those who have not experienced it.

- Anon

992. Concealed talent brings no reputation.

- Anon

993. Difficulties are things that show a person what they are.

- Epictetus

994. The hood does not make the monk.
- Siddhartha Gautama

995. What is right and what is practical are two different things."

- James Buchanan

996. To vote is like the payment of a debt, a duty never to be neglected, if its performance is possible.

- Rutherford B. Hayes

997. If you can't stand the heat, get out of the kitchen.

- Harry S. Truman

998. Give every man thy ear, but few thy voice.
- William Shakespeare

999. Uneasy lies the head that wears a crown.
- William Shakespeare

1000. It is impossible to begin to learn that which one thinks one already knows.
- Epictetus